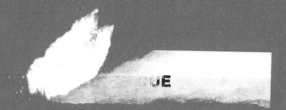

UE

What is a Wookiee?

Senior Editor Tori Kosara
Designer Mark Richards
Pre-production Producer Marc Staples
Senior Producer Alex Bell
Managing Editor Laura Gilbert
Managing Art Editor Maxine Pedliham
Art Director Lisa Lanzarini
Publisher Julie Ferris
Publishing Director Simon Beecroft

For Lucasfilm
Executive Editor Jonathan W. Rinzler
Art Director Troy Alders
Story Group Rayne Roberts, Pablo Hidalgo, Leland Chee

Reading Consultant
Dr. Linda Gambrell, PhD

First published in the United States in 2015 by
DK Publishing
4th Floor, 345 Hudson Street, New York 10014

10 9 8 7 6 5 4 3 2 1
001-SD174-Feb/15

Published in Great Britain by Dorling Kindersley Limited.

A catalog record for this book
is available from the Library of Congress.

ISBN: 978-1-4654-3385-5 (Hardback)
ISBN: 978-1-4654-3386-2 (Paperback)

Printed and bound in China by South China Printing Company Ltd.

www.starwars.com
www.dk.com

A WORLD OF IDEAS:
SEE ALL THERE IS TO KNOW

Contents

C-3PO

My name is C-3PO.

I am a droid.

I am a talking machine.

I live far, far away in space.

Lots of creatures live here.

I will be telling you about
some of them.

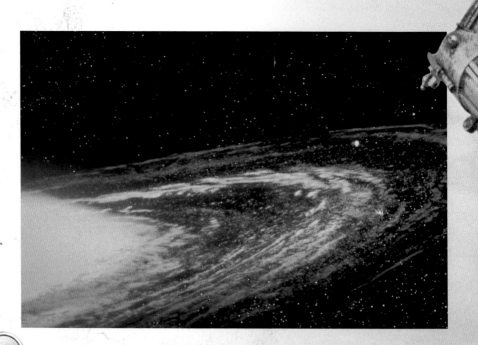

Over the Years

I have been on many adventures in my life. My body has not always looked the same. Now, I look very different from when I was first built by a young boy.

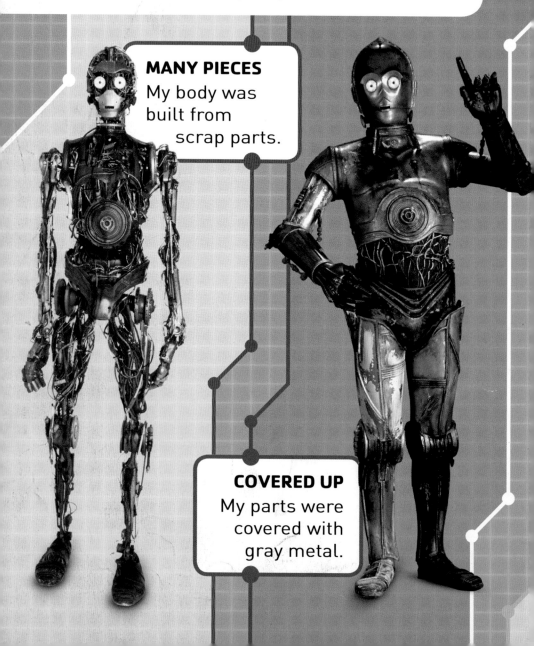

MANY PIECES
My body was built from scrap parts.

COVERED UP
My parts were covered with gray metal.

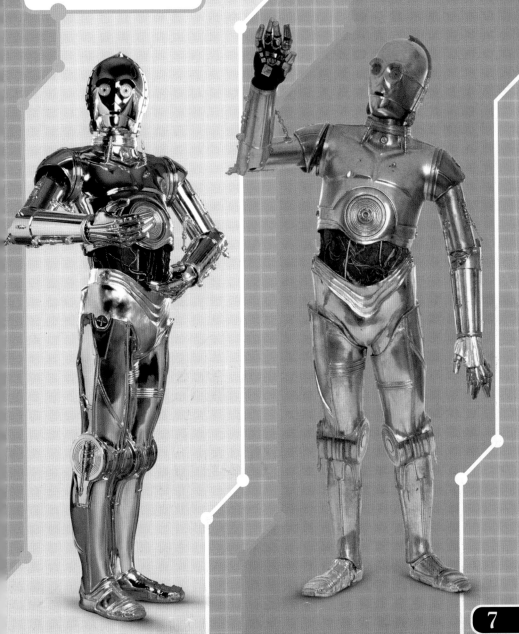

GOLDEN SHINE
I got shiny gold plating many years later.

WEAR AND TEAR
Later, some of my parts needed to be replaced.

Aliens

Some creatures in the galaxy
are aliens.
There are lots of
different aliens.
Aliens are not human.

Humans also live here—
my friend Padmé is a human.

R2-D2

This is my friend R2-D2.

He is a droid, too.

R2-D2 likes talking.
His voice sounds like
whistles and beeps,
but I can
understand
him.

R2-D2 is a clever little machine.
He has all sorts of useful tools.
R2-D2 can fix anything!

Chewbacca

Meet Chewbacca.

He is a tall, furry alien called
a Wookiee.

He is the best friend of Han Solo,
who is a human.

They fly a spaceship together.

Sometimes, I ride with them!

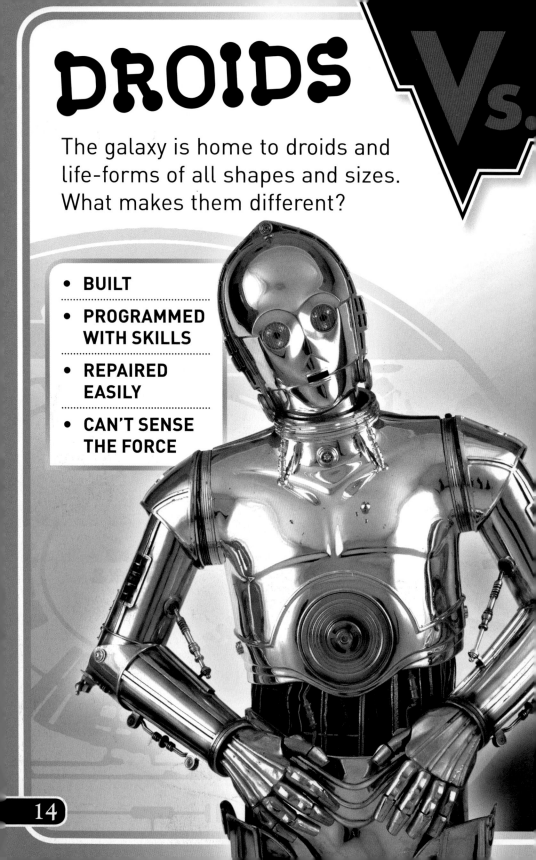

DROIDS

Vs.

The galaxy is home to droids and life-forms of all shapes and sizes. What makes them different?

- **BUILT**
- **PROGRAMMED WITH SKILLS**
- **REPAIRED EASILY**
- **CAN'T SENSE THE FORCE**

LIFE-FORMS

- BORN
- MUST LEARN SKILLS
- HEAL SLOWLY
- CAN SENSE THE FORCE

Jar Jar Binks

Now say hello to Jar Jar Binks.

He is a friendly alien.

Jar Jar comes from
an underwater city.

On land, Jar Jar is
always falling over!

He has a very long
pink tongue.

Watto

Let's visit Watto's shop.

Watto is a blue alien.

He has a bad temper.

Watto flies around

using the wings on his back.

He sells bits of old machines

called junk.

WATTO'S SHOP

HoloNews took a look inside Watto's shop. You can buy parts here for the right price.

Droids

Find the right model for you. **Prices vary.**

A HOLONEWS SPECIAL!

Podracing equipment

POWER PLUG
Every Podracer needs one to make it to the finish line. **595 coins**

Tools

SOCKET SPANNER
This wrench can fix anything.
Just 20 coins

HYDROSPANNER
The perfect tool for all your needs. *Only 75 coins*

Spare parts

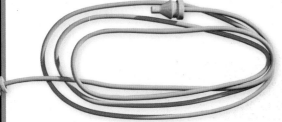

POWER CABLE
Power up with the right cord.
Prices vary.

**NO MONEY,
NO PARTS, NO DEAL!**

No credit chips! Cash only.

Sebulba

Now it's time to meet Sebulba.
This nasty alien races in
a vehicle called a Podracer.
He likes to go fast.
Sebulba will do anything to win.
He will even throw things
at other Podracers!

Pit Droids

Pit droids fix the Podracers.
They are very useful and can
carry heavy things.
Pit droids sometimes
get into trouble.
There is one way to stop them.
Tap them on the nose
and they fold up.

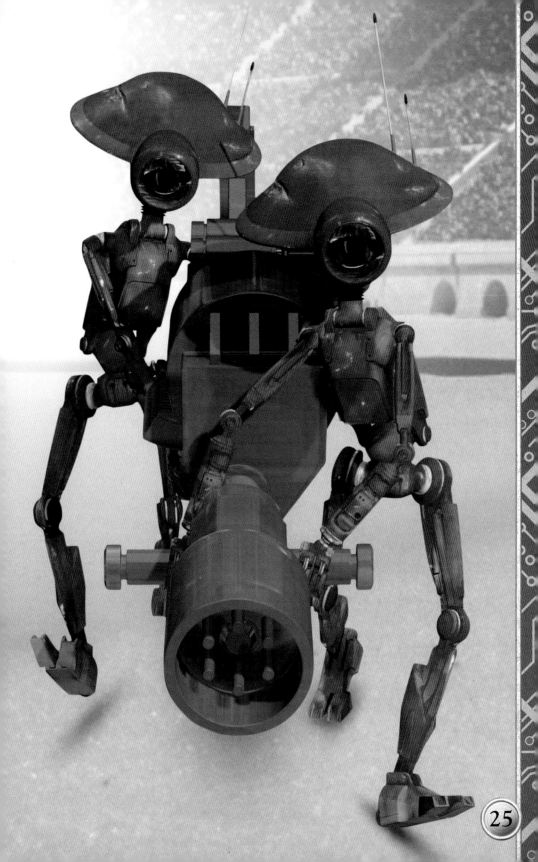

How to Activate a Pit Droid

Pit droids can help with simple jobs. They fold up so that they can be stored and kept out of trouble. It is easy to wake a pit droid. Just follow these simple steps.

Tap here

Droid unfolds

Legs activate

STEP **1**

STEP **2**

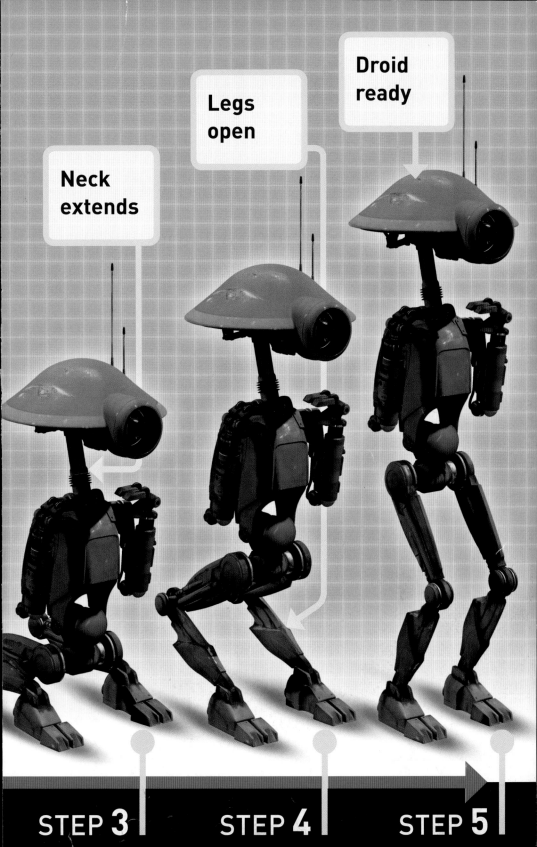

Neck extends

Legs open

Droid ready

STEP **3**

STEP **4**

STEP **5**

Jabba the Hutt

Jabba the Hutt is a nasty alien.

He has a fat body and a long tail.

His body is covered in sticky slime.

Jabba's eyes are red and yellow
and his breath is smelly.
Don't get too near him!

Dexter Jettster

Let's visit Dexter Jettster's restaurant.

This friendly alien has four arms.

Dexter is a great cook.

He cooks the food at Dex's Diner.

Should we find out what's on the menu?

Dex's DINER

CoCo Town, Coruscant
555-4321

 Credit chips accepted here

MAIN MEAL

Shawda club sandwich

This is a delicious sandwich. It is served on toasted or therm-zapped bread.

6.7 credits

DESSERT

Sic-Six-layer cake

A popular dessert from Sisk. This cake has many different colored layers.

2.5 credits
(served by the slice)

★★★

DRINK

photon fizzle

A tasty green fizzy drink
1.7 credits

The best food this side of the Senate District!

Lizard Keepers

These creatures are lizard keepers.
They live in big holes in
the ground.
Sometimes, the lizard keepers
ride around on giant lizards.
The lizards are good at jumping
and climbing.

Jawas

Jawas are small creatures with shiny yellow eyes.
Their faces are hidden under the hoods of their brown cloaks.

These little aliens find droids and
bits of machines to sell.
Once, they even sold R2-D2!

How to Choose the Perfect Droid

Buying a used droid could save you money. Make sure you choose your droid carefully. This guide tells you how to find the right droid for you.

1 See everything first

Look closely at all the droids.

2 Ask where it is from

The trader should know where the droid came from.

3 | Take a close look

Watch out for problems, such as broken parts and loose wires.

4 | Return if faulty

Make sure that you can return the droid if something goes wrong.

Yoda

Yoda is very old and very wise.
He has green skin and
big, pointy ears.

No one knows what kind
of creature he is or
where he comes from.
Yoda is a skilled warrior.
He uses a green lightsaber
during battles.

Ewoks

If we go deep into the forest,
we may meet my friends the Ewoks.
Ewoks are small, furry creatures.
They live in houses that they
build high up in the trees.

I hope you
have enjoyed
learning about
the creatures
in my galaxy.

Goodbye!

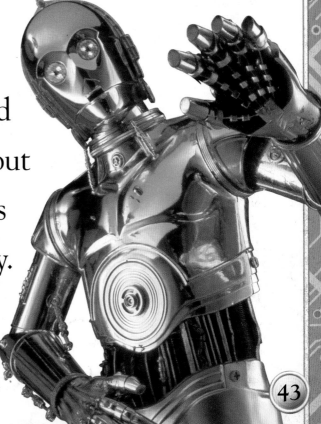

Glossary

Alien
From a country or place different from one's own.

Creature
An animal that is not a human being.

Droid
A kind of robot. C-3PO is a droid.

Forest
A large area covered with trees and smaller plants.

Hood
A covering for the head and neck that has an opening for the face.

Lizard
A reptile with a long body, a tail, four legs, and scaly, rough, or spiny skin.

Plating
An outer covering made of metal.

Podracer
A vehicle used for racing on the planet Tatooine.

Spaceship
A vehicle used for traveling in space.

Wing
A part of an animal that allows it to fly.

Index

Guide for Parents

DK Readers is a multi-level interactive reading adventure series for children, developing the habit of reading widely for both pleasure and information. These books have an exciting running text interspersed with a range of reading genres to suit your child's reading ability, as required by the school curriculum. Each book is designed to develop your child's reading skills, fluency, grammar awareness, and comprehension in order to build confidence and engagement when reading.

Ready for a *Beginning to Read* book
YOUR CHILD SHOULD

- be familiar with using beginning letter sounds and context clues to figure out unfamiliar words.
- be aware of the need for a slight pause at commas and a longer one at periods.
- alter his/her expression for questions and exclamations.

A valuable and shared reading experience

For many children, reading requires much effort, but adult participation can make this both fun and easier. So here are a few tips on how to use this book with your child.

TIP 1 **Check out the contents together before your child begins:**

- read the text about the book on the back cover.
- flip through the book and and stop to chat about the contents page together to heighten your child's interest and expectation.
- make use of unfamiliar or difficult words on the page in a brief discussion.
- chat about the non-fiction reading features used in the book, such as headings, captions, recipes, lists or charts.

TIP 2 Support your child as he/she reads the story pages:

- give the book to your child to read and turn the pages.

- where necessary, encourage your child to break a word into syllables, sound out each one, and then flow the syllables together. Ask him/her to reread the sentence to check the meaning.

- when there's a question mark or an exclamation mark, encourage your child to vary his/her voice as he/she reads the sentence. Demonstrate how to do this if it is helpful.

TIP 3 Chat at the end of each page:

- the factual pages tend to be more difficult than the story pages, and are designed to be shared with your child.

- ask questions about the text and the meaning of the words used. These help to develop comprehension skills and awareness of the language used.

A FEW ADDITIONAL TIPS

- Always encourage your child to try reading difficult words by themselves. Praise any self-corrections, for example, "I like the way you sounded out that word and then changed the way you said it, to make sense."

- Try to read together everyday. Reading little and often is best. These books are divided into manageable chapters for one reading session. However, after 10 minutes, only keep going if your child wants to read on.

- Read other books of different types to your child just for enjoyment and information.

Series consultant, **Dr. Linda Gambrell,** Distinguished Professor of Education at Clemson University, has served as President of the National Reading Conference, the College Reading Association, and the International Reading Association. She is also reading consultant for the **DK Adventures.**

Have you read these other great books from DK?

BEGINNING TO READ

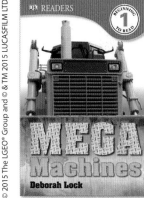

Visit the planet Tatooine, and meet many people and creatures.

Join Luke Skywalker and his friends on their adventures.

Hard hats on! Watch the machines build a new school.

BEGINNING TO READ ALONE

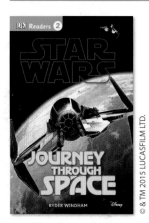

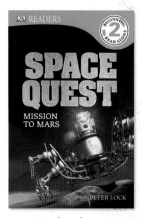

Explore the amazing planets and moons in the *Star Wars*® galaxy.

Meet a band of rebels, brave enough to take on the Empire!

Embark on a mission to space, and explore Mars.